Contents

Words shown in **bold** in the text are explained in the glossary.

All the places in this book are shown on the map on page 22.

The Clothes We Wear

From T-shirts, jeans and hats, to jumpers, coats, dresses and scarves – every day, we all wear clothes.

On hot days, we choose clothes that keep us cool.

On cold days, we choose clothes that keep us warm.

We choose our clothes to show what's important to us.

We choose clothes that show who we are.

We wear clothes that show what we believe.

Dressed for School

Every morning, children wake up and get dressed for school.

Some put on a school uniform, while others can choose what clothes to wear.

On the school bus in the United States

Off to school in the city of Nairobi in Kenya

Many children in the United Kingdom wear a school uniform.

These girls go to school in Malaysia.

These school uniforms in Brazil show off the colours of the country's flag.

These children are on their way to school in India.

Colourful Quechua Clothes

High in the Andes Mountains in Peru, Quechua people raise sheep, alpacas and llamas.

They use the wool from their animals to make clothes.

The wool is dyed many colours.

Then people **weave** and knit the wool to make skirts, jackets and *ponchos*.

A Quechua woman weaving with wool

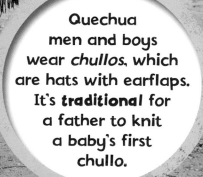

An alpaca

A chullo

A poncho

Sandals made from recycled tyres

Quechua men and boys wear *chullos*, which are hats with earflaps. It's **traditional** for a father to knit a baby's first chullo.

9

Clothes from Reindeer

When you live in a place that's much colder than the inside of a freezer, how do you keep warm?

Nenets people in Siberia wear coats and boots made from reindeer skins and fur.

A reindeer skin coat may have a hood and sleeves with built-in gloves.

Reindeer skin boots reach right to the tops of a person's legs.

The Nenets are reindeer **herders**. They move from place to place finding food for their animals.

A tent, called a *chum*, made from reindeer skins

A Nenets boy wearing a reindeer skin coat

Beautiful Saris

In India, women and girls have worn saris for more than 2000 years.

A sari is a long piece of brightly coloured cloth.

A sari is draped, or wrapped, around the body to give many different looks.

These girls are wearing highly decorative saris at a festival.

Embroidery

Some saris are plain, while others are decorated with **embroidery**, beads and even tiny mirrors. A sari can be up to 8 m long.

Under a sari, women and girls wear a long skirt.

They also wear a short, tight-fitting blouse called a *choli*.

These women wear saris to go to work on a farm.

13

Traditional Clothes

Sometimes we wear traditional or special clothes to celebrate a festival.

Some traditional costumes look like the clothes our **ancestors** wore.

These boys are dancing at a folk festival in Bulgaria.

These girls are at a festival on the island of Tenerife, Spain.

14

Every year, hundreds of Native American **powwows** are held across North America. At a powwow, Native people wear traditional clothes and perform traditional songs and dances.

Fantastic Headdresses

The Long Horn Miao people live in China.

For special occasions and festivals, women and girls wear dramatic headdresses.

To create her headdress, a girl attaches a pair of wooden horns to her head.

Wooden horns

Then a large bundle of fabric, black wool and real hair is tied to the horns.

This girl's mother is helping her make her headdress.

16

Long Horn Miao women never cut their long hair. The real hair in a girl's headdress is from her female ancestors.

Maasai Clothes

The Maasai people of Kenya and Tanzania wear clothes in very bright colours – especially red.

A shuka

Maasai people wear a blanket, or cloak, around their shoulders.

The cloak is called a *shuka*.

A shuka might be just one colour, or it could have a striped or checked pattern.

The colour red is very special to the Maasai people. They believe that red helps to keep them safe from wild animals such as lions.

Maasai boys wearing shukas

A beaded collar

Maasai people wear lots of jewellery made of beads.

Sandals made from car tyres

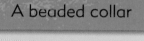

Ankle bracelet

All Around the World

What piece of clothing do children around the world wear to school, at playtime, for sport and even to bed?

It's the T-shirt!

Sometimes a favourite T-shirt gets too small, so you might give it to a **charity**. Then the charity might send it to another country where children need clothes. Soon it will be another kid's favourite T-shirt!

Nepal

Ecuador

Australia

Vietnam

Canada

Ghana

21

Where in the World?

Canada
Pages 4 and 21

Tenerife, Spain
Page 14

United Kingdom
Page 7

Bulgaria
Page 14

Israel
Page 5

Nepal
Page 20

Siberia, Russia
Pages 10–11

China
Pages 16–17

North America

Europe

Asia

United States
Pages 6 and 15

Africa

South America

Vietnam
Page 21

Ecuador
Page 20

Ghana
Page 21

India
Pages 7 and 12–13

Australia

Peru
Pages 8–9

Argentina
Page 4

Brazil
Page 7

Tanzania
Pages 18–19

Kenya
Pages 5 and 6

Australia
Pages 4 and 20

Malaysia
Pages 5 and 7

Glossary

ancestor
A relative who lived a long time ago. For example, your great-grandparents and great-great-grandparents are your ancestors.

charity
An organisation that raises money and uses it to do good work such as helping people living in poverty.

embroidery
Creating a picture or pattern on a piece of cloth by making many small stitches with thread.

herder
A person who herds, or moves, animals from place to place so that the animals can find food.

powwow
A ceremony in North America where large numbers of Native people, usually from many tribes, gather to feast, dance, sing and honour the traditions of their ancestors.

traditional
Something that has been done in a certain way for many years by a group of people.

weave
To make fabric from long pieces of wool by tightly threading, or weaving, them together.

Index

Learn More Online

To learn more about clothes
around the world, go to
www.rubytuesdaybooks.com/clothes